Mar

SIMPLE HAPPY

A Collection of Poetry

By S. C. Porter

ISBN: 9798394348044 (Paperback)

Book Design by Lauren Yates/Arete Graphix
Book edited by Kristine Hutchinson

Printed in the United States of America

First printing edition 2023

Published by Porter Publishing Co.
Wilmington, NC

SIMPLE HAPPY

A Collection of Poetry

This book is dedicated to the girl who thought she couldn't,
but then, she fucking did.

And to Wyatt, Lincoln, and Michael.
Thank you for giving me the best kind of simple happy.
The effortless kind.
I love you.

Please note: while it may seem that these poems are about
one specific person, they may or may not be.
These poems represent my deepest feelings, but also may
represent feelings of
family and friends along the way that helped me get through
a difficult time, because they
too, had been there. Any correlation or connection made
regarding someone you may assume a poem is
about should be taken lightly.

Dear Reader,

For the past year, I've journaled to allow my heart to heal, to expose pieces of me I didn't know were hanging by loosened threads and being sewn back together at the same time, until I compiled those words into a collection of what eventually became the collection of poetry you're about to read.

It holds secrets, truths, admissions, and fantasies of mine. It's raw, emotional, and, at times, downright devastating. But, through these pages, please know that at the end of each passage, I felt happy.

No matter what has happened, I am happy.

I learned a lot this year about myself. About what makes me happy and what doesn't.

When I think about you reading this collection of words, I patiently wait to hear what you think, how you can relate, and how it maybe helps to explain some of the confusing times you may be navigating, too.

Life is funny that way — so weird and confusing. It can be mean. It can be cruel.

But, it also can be wonderful and lovely and rewarding after times of weirdness, confusion, and devastation.

I implore you to go into this book, ready to mess it up. Please write down thoughts as they come to your mind. Use it as a journal, too. Jot down memories in the empty spaces of each page. Annotate, highlight, tab, and share it with your family, your friends. Maybe one day, even your enemy.

While I've shared a little of what I went through last year on social media, many of you related to even just the minute things and general tidbits I shared, and you poured your heart out to me. For that, I thank you. Your messages sometimes brought tears to my eyes. It reminded me that we are never alone in our sadness, especially in our grief or moments of madness, if not sometimes extended.

Sometimes, it's nice to hear that we are not the only ones who suffer inside—a trick to human nature's guise. The habit to form would be recognizing it. And, to get out of it, I suppose.

If you are going through something, I write to you as a reminder to seek help and a friend before you let it take away all the simple kinds of happy you may miss out on if you don't. If only for a time, let it go.

For so long, I lay in bed, sick, feeling sorry for myself, and after some time, I decided I deserved to be happy again.

And, so you do.

Author's Note

I decided to write this section *last* but put it first.
Let me tell you why.

Because when I first started writing this collection of words, I was in the thick of it all, the worst parts of my life so far, and months later, in fact... just *one* year later, I am in such a different place. This section of this book looked very different back then. And I'm writing this now because after that time passed, I went back and read what once was here in this space, and it didn't make any sense for me to keep.

I simply hit *delete.*

Suddenly, it dawned on me that when I finished writing *Simple Happy*, my moments of extreme grief, worrying madness, immense pain, and overwhelming sadness were just brief periods in my life.

It made me think.

In just a year, how much do our lives change? For the good or the bad. I have learned after stepping back and taking a deeper look, that when terrible things happen to us, we can either let it all but consume us, or we can choose to take the things that *happen* to us and turn them into moments we *take* from, that we can gain from... that we can grow from.

What I mean by that is we can let moments of true sadness envelope us, swallow us whole like an ocean mindlessly eats a raindrop. Or, we can simply allow those moments to be just small moments in the linear span of time. We can *take* from those moments instead of allowing them to continue to take from us.

When I sit and think about my life and the things that I have created, I begin to understand that at times when I really needed *me*, I let tragedy, hate, and hopelessness fill my heart because I felt like something was missing. I felt disposable. I let deep, unrooted sadness engulf me, and I think the most important thing I can do in the aftermath is flush it out. Be rid of the intermingling thoughts that could completely cover me and change my happy being.

I used to think nothing could change that about me, my happiness. How naive, I know now. I began writing *Simple Happy* as an outlet. I was changed in the middle of it. And then, by the end, a completely different person altogether. Maybe by taking in some of these words that helped me get through it can be an outlet for you, too.

A year later, I somehow am *okay*. I somehow feel good. I somehow feel welcoming to life's hardships. Because, after all, isn't that where we grow? Aren't hard, all-too-moving things, what shapes beautiful things? I wrote that out in another book once before.

When I first sat down to write *Simple Happy*, I had this very one-sided version of what happiness meant. I have had a shaded experience of "happiness" in my life. Sometimes, it can be very confusing, the things that make me happy. And, I think it took something even more daunting to bring up all the yuck in my life that I somehow had missed, buried, and possibly ignored completely.

Is that what we do? Do we hide behind shades and screens to put on a show for those who look into our lives? Do we showcase all the goodness covered in filters, hoping no one notices the bad or undesirable? Do we somehow trick our minds into believing something that isn't real, all so we can pretend we are happy?

When I started typing words for this book, I was in a place in my life where I thought if someone wanted to know how to be happy, they should take it from me. In other people's opinion, I was a walking portrait of happiness. Everything in my life seemed ideal and *the goal*.

I heard it all the time.

I still hear it.

But life and the universe, of course, had their way with me, showing me, as my former therapist once told me, "*You're not as powerful as you think.*"

What is happiness?

Over the past year, I became obsessed with the concept of happiness. It was all I could think about. I constantly thought to myself, *I fucking deserve to be happy again.* No one could possibly tell me any differently. I started to really look into every aspect of my life, trying to pinpoint every moment I felt happy, when it would happen, why it would happen, and how I could make it happen over and over again. I think my reason for this was that I kept being drawn back to the past and its mistakes, and those around me wouldn't allow me to move on, no matter how badly I wanted to.

Let me ask you a question. Do you know what makes *you* happy? Like, that true, unadulterated, undeniable, good, meaningful happiness?

How does one achieve it? Where does it stem from? Can you find it easily? Is it possible it's now our life's mission? Will it take a lifetime to achieve?

Sometimes, life is hard. Every person on this planet knows this. Sometimes, we know it can be "unhappy." Filled with moments so completely full of bullshit and terrifying decisions to be made. There are forks in the road, and each one might look exactly the same. Each one can possibly look like the *right* decision, or maybe they all look different and look like the *wrong* decision, and you begin to settle into another daunting, confused state.

After reading *Simple Happy*, I implore you to dive deeper into your own version of happiness. However different it may look from everyone else's version, please. Chase it. And chase it until you can no longer run.

Will you take joy in the simple things from now on? In the ways you really wished you could have last year? And this year, did it just come faster than you could say *slow down...*

Will you fight harder for the life you wanted last year? Will you stop waiting for tomorrow in the ways you used to? Ask yourself, *why not now*? What stops you from stepping out the door instead of staying inside, hidden from the version you want to be? He or she is tired of waiting.

One thing I've learned in life is never to compare the beginning of your journey to the middle of someone else's. We all have to get there in our own time. No one can pick us up and plop us into the *Happy*. I've learned the hard way that only I can do that for myself. There's no way someone can just grant that to me. I have to seek it. I have to be the one to grab it.

If you asked me today, I have about ten solid things to describe who I am. These things are what I've come to know as my *Identity*.

I am forgiving. I am a mother. I am a lover. I am a fighter. I am a seeker. And so on... I am these things with all that I am. I can tell you exactly who I am, where I'm going, and who I want to be. Do I know the exact path I will ultimately take to get there? No. I don't think anyone does, considering life has a funny way of showing us where we're going. We cannot predict the future or the hardships we will face. We cannot predict our health years from now or financial gains or losses. But we do have a lot of control over how we see ourselves. We have control over who we want to be. We have a lot of control over how people treat us. We can control what expectations we set for ourselves in terms of where we want to be in life. If we can define these things, if we can define how someone treats us, where we want to be, and who we want to be, I truly think we can define how to get *Happy*. If we clearly define our goals, we can set pathways to achieve them.

First of all, we have to define what makes us happy. After all, to know how to get happy, we must know what helps to obtain it. We must also figure out the best ways to avoid depleting it.

How do you find happiness? Who do you feel happiest around? What gives you your best feelings of happiness after being surrounded by it? The same goes for being completely open to seeing what is draining you. Where are your sources of feeling unhappy coming from?

Here's a start to being happy.
Your relationships.

Take advantage of the good relationships you have in your life right now. Don't wait. Spend time with the people that bring you joy. Reach out and set aside time for those you love being around. I truly believe the best way to start on our happy journey is to be surrounded by genuinely good people who are also looking for *Happy.* Go to lunch. Catch up. Invite a friend or family member for charcuterie and a glass of wine. Extend a hand. Write a handwritten note to someone you're thinking about. It takes two minutes and costs a stamp.

How about we start talking better to ourselves? It's, after all, the most important relationship to care for and give attention to. The great Jim Carey has said *it doesn't take much to feel good about yourself.*

It's the little things. How about we start reading what we want to read?

I know this book will not be for everyone, simply because I know from personal experience that I was in denial about many things I've now come to terms with. I was in denial about some of the ways I was living my life. I've reflected and spent a lot of time with these thoughts. I judged myself and created this book based on those instances that I now realize and, in foresight, could have done better.

Create many places where you could sit in your home and find peace. Places you can meditate. Places you can reflect. Even so, places you can *scream*. We all need a good scream every once in a while. To let out frustrations, normal emotions we all feel from time to time. And sometimes, it helps to have them in different places of the home so that you can reach out and utilize those spaces as quickly as you need them. Create them indoors. Create them outdoors.

Sometimes, it's very easy to find a happy place. You just have to seek it, right? I love a good thrift shop. They are the most effective place to get beautiful China for literally a dollar a piece. I also like shopping end-of-season sales. Stocking up for the holidays and thinking ahead to next year is something my mother and I have in common. Pottery Barn typically is very pricey. But at the end of the season, everything is 50% off. I love racking up on Christmas items for next year and saving on purchases at the end of the day. It's the little things we tend to find joy in. The holidays make me so happy. It doesn't have to come few and far between. It can happen more often than not, only if you let it.

Do not get comfortable in unhappiness
There is a reservation in a still-quiet
Where your water flourishes
Don't place your happiness in others
But in yourself, first and foremost

It is quite possible that you can find a bigger happiness in doing the little things that cause a slight moment of profound togetherness over and over again. Find the things that make you happy, even if only slightly. Even if it's just for a small moment in time. Just like small habits forming into larger, better habits... small moments of *Happy* again and again are what you should strive for. A hot cup of your favorite tea. A mid-afternoon stroll in the warm sunshine, the breeze flitting your hair over your shoulder. Those moments will make you happy, I'm telling you. Not an expensive car, not a big home, and certainly not any other material thing you can't talk to when the doors are closed and no one is watching.

Create memories while walking in your neighborhood with your children. Or book a trip near a faraway friend. Stay with that friend to save on a hotel. Go outside. Breathe in fresh air.

Before reading this book, take a moment to use this page or a journal to write down five ways you find happiness throughout your day. And reflect on how you can add more...

I ask myself this now:
"What is your happiness?"

Where does it come from
Why does it come
Why does it stay away for brief moments of time
Happiness is the inner calm found
When I am not wanting more
Not justifying wants when my mind runs wild
Simply just being okay with where I stand
And how I got there

Darling girl, if I could go back, I'd tell you not to get lost in the things that almost kill you now, for defeat comes all on its own when your happiness returns as your enemies still frown...

I am at peace with how I left things with you
It's not my responsibility to hold you accountable
Not when you fail at keeping score for yourself
Only holding me to the standard
I smile at the grace I gave to you
It's nice knowing I gave it my all
When at the time
You tried taking everything I ever had
Sometimes you still do
You're not for me
I am all I could ever need
At all
Ever
I don't look to you anymore for happiness
You are not a good example

I am the example

I choose to be happy
I am not looking to you to pick me up

What in the world do they do to us
How do they have so much hold on us
How long is this going to go on
Not anymore
I choose my path

Not you
I am the one who grasps my dreams
Turns them into actual things that I can say I've done
I will plot all of my actions
And you will watch from a distance as I move on
No longer crying a tear for you
But crying many tears at the happiness
I give to myself
I have made it a habit to smile at myself in the mirror
Every morning and say out loud
You are more than enough
So much more than you could possibly know
If they see it
So should you
Go easy on yourself
Plant a seed to be kinder to those wrinkles
I know it's hard but
They didn't get there from unhappy memories
You got them from laughing with your children
You got them from smiling so big
Not even the clouds could have dampened that sunshine
I wish you the exact love I feel for him today
No matter what you have done to me

I forgive you
If only so I can sleep peacefully at night
For half a year
Six long months
Too many days and nights and more days
I starved my bones of the smallest amount of meat they have
Ever carried
Then I snapped the fuck out of it
Mostly because I missed eating
And you weren't worth my sternum showing through the
Thin skin on my chest
Many moving rivers I cried
Rough and violent
Like a sea that could swallow entire ships
And when I realized that even rough seas eventually calm
I accepted my fate and dried like an African desert
In my moments of true angst, I must remember
It won't always be this way
It doesn't have to stay this way
It won't always be
This
Way

The short moments in time with you are spans of oceans
They spread out so far
Wider than any sea you could find on a map
But then you always leave
You pull in your love
A tide that is never predictable
Confusing the clocks
And you leave a bath of tears instead
Once again
I'm empty
Dried like an ancient river
Speckled with dirt, but nothing shiny
You could not possibly be the happiness
You once were for me
And that's okay
Times changes things

I don't want to hold in anger toward you
For that anger will rot away the little happiness I still have
I look forward to
The direction I move
I will dive into it with my whole heart
That's what I'll do
In my loss of you
I gained so much more of me
I see with two eyes now
Not one angry one
In the middle of my forehead
Once so bold and terrifying
She could have killed
I hold him with both arms now
Tighter than I've ever held onto anything
And to think, I thought you were the one
The grief I experience will one day give me wings to fly
I hold onto a hope that I'll float away from the ledge
Not jump

-There's happiness in not giving up

I used to lay in those sheets for days

Days
Upon
Days
Upon
Days

Sad with aching, red eyes
No food in me
Unable to understand the amount of pain you left there
In the pit of my empty stomach
Remember when my mother had to take care of our
Children because I simply couldn't

Don't forget
I'll remind you every time

Now, the bed has become my sanctuary
Where happiness begins and ends in the same place

-There is happiness in how he lays where you left me

Worrying about the things you took from me yesterday
Only takes away the kindness in my heart I have to give away
Tomorrow
So no
You cannot take anything else from me
Especially the love I have to give away to him
Maybe it was always meant to be his anyway
I dream of the ring he will someday give to me as I think
About consigning yours
It's so sad that shiny things can still shine even when you
Dulled away The meaning of them
You won't take my happy any longer
He gives me too much to be sad anymore
Yesterday weighed the amount of a thousand yesterdays
I so easily want to give you up
If only it means that my happiness can return
If only it means I don't cry myself to sleep anymore
If only I stop seeing her car around town and behind
My eyelids every single time they fall
Now I'm lucky
Because I only see what's in front of me
His old truck in the drive

I am capable of the most belligerent cry
Yet the tears don't fall from my eyes anymore for you
How beautiful that time was
Looks like I know that now
When I knew nothing of myself anymore
I became so far from me that I lost my own beauty
My eyes so red and full of puff that I looked so unlike myself

I resembled a beaten fruit
Now I am a ray of sunshine
I am a big girl
I don't let your small things get in my way

-There's happiness that comes from knowing I'm the bigger
person

It's funny how things pan out
Isn't it
Like how you said you'd be the best I would ever have
And now I have
Better

It's funny how things slide out
Isn't it
Like how the truth just fell from your lips as I pulled
And pulled
You made me feel like the manipulator
Even though it was always you.

I left you
All while I still had my dignity intact
The grace I left at your feet should get you through
The next 40 years of your life
Hopefully you won't miss me too much

-There's happiness in letting go of what is no longer mine

I do not have to stay married to you
Eight months down
Four to go

How cruel of the state to make me stay bound
To you longer than I should want to

Should you always remember that ugly things
Can turn beautiful too
Like a stab wound that can become a moon-shaped scar
Like the one I gave myself on my palm the night I
Found out about *her*
Reminding me of what I survived
Should the ugly show us that sometimes
Suffering is necessary
It's a part of the war
That to win
You must have killed and almost been killed
I can let you go
I can become my own heart
One
Not part of two
I can stand alone on my own two feet
For you are not the one
And that is fucking okay
I am not supposed to be tied to you in this way
I am supposed to have my own back
Not yours

-There is happiness in fighting a battle you're meant to win

Their laughter reminds me that two good things came from
All of those years of
Pretending
At least that's what I tell myself
Was I so blinded by the love I thought we had
That I shielded away from the only light that could
Help me see
You no longer have a hold on me
You cannot manipulate the sky not to let down the rain
It falls on its own
No help needed
Nothing could have held back that kind of downfall
Not even you

Finally, I chose myself

I chose my happiness
Over yours

I was lost simply because you took me
A kidnapping of sorts with no blue lights turned on
A rouse
A taking in the middle of the night
My complete sadness you doused us in
A scream so loud in the middle of the night
With a knife in my hand
No understanding of how it ended up there
Did it wake the children
My scream
It surely didn't wake you
You stayed asleep
But still with a watchful eye
You let me die there on the floor as I learned you had
Another *her*

-There is happiness in learning

The dogwood trees in the backyard bloomed their white
Poofs of hope
The week I sold the home we built together
Just two years before
Then
I posted a video
Me cleaning out that gift you gave
That constant reminder of what was
And it paid for me to move on
Sometimes
In life
The hardest things we go through
Somehow
In the end
Bring us peace

-There is happiness in selling that thing you gave me

I wish you the best
Because we both deserve that
No matter what has happened
I'll not forget the good times
We shared
It's okay it ended
And it's okay it began way back when
I meant it

Never be so polite, you forget your power

Never wield such power, you forget to be polite

And if I didn't know better

I'd think you were listening to me now

What died didn't stay dead

What died didn't stay dead

You're alive

You're alive in my head

—Taylor

There is a peace in my heart
My every waking moment
Pretty much because
I fucking let that shit go
There is no perfect life waiting for any of us
There is no right time to do that thing you want to do
It's time for peace, my dear friend
Invite it

-There is happiness in letting shit go

I will not focus on you
I should focus on me
I'm the one left behind
I am the only one who can save me
Not you
So
That is what I will do
I will be there for me
I will save me
I will love me
I will talk kindly to me
Me
Me
Me
The one you left behind while you tried to save yourself
But miserably failed to
Because it was always me that was meant to save you
Not the other way around

-There is happiness in Me

Pretty girl
You're more than the labels they place upon you
You are more than the money in your bank account
You are more than the dollars you make for someone else
Pretty girl
Do you know your power
Do you know the hold you have on yourself
Let it go
Free yourself from the bounds you see
There are many more that are invisible
Pretty girl
See the beauty in all things
Even the things that keep you sad
You don't have to stay that way
I promise

You can be strong when you're weak
You can stand tall when you're only five feet in height
Remember the stars didn't get there overnight
I welcome saying goodbye to things that don't entice
My Dreams
And so if I have to say goodbye to you
So be it

Tomorrow is **not** an excuse

I'll document today

The love I have for you now

I'll put down my work

The things that take me away from you

The things I continue to do instead of playing with you

You beg at my feet and sometimes I don't even listen

Sometimes I feel the need to make money for you instead of

The need to make you love me

But today

Right now

I'll take the time to show you

You're the most important project of my life

You're my most precious work

The art to be displayed in my museum

The things I show off

Take pride in

The only thing I really need

And together, we will walk in the sunshine

We will search for pine cones

We will play with our farm of dogs

And laugh until our bellies full of popsicles hurt

You're what I should be focusing on when you're next to me

For one day, I will look up...
And you won't want to play with me anymore
You'll stop begging at my feet for the attention you deserve
You'll want it from someone else
And all you will remember is me working
And that to me
Would be the biggest regret of my life

-There is happiness in our children. Play with them *now.*

There are ways to do that thing you love every single day
You don't have to go a day without it
Remember that

There's no magic ticket pulling me from this hell
There's not a pill that will cure the sadness
It was me who wiped the sadness from my eyes
It was an unbearable time I was forced to embrace in
It was traveling the road of grief alone
Before I realized I never needed you
I needed me

No

I will not be silent

To appease you

To make it so that people don't see who you really are

To calm your anxiety

To lessen the hurt you irresponsibly toss around

No

I will not stop shouting

From the rooftops

In an attempt to lessen your consequences and

No

I will not be gaslighted into thinking

The betrayal you inhabit

In your bones

Is anything other than

Being tied to envy

And greed and pure disloyalty

I am not selfish, not hateful

I am just protecting

ME

-There is happiness in letting them know when enough is
enough

There is no shame in
Starting over
Leaving him
Wanting more for yourself
Giving more than they deserved
Hoping for better days
Starving yourself while the world entirely starved you
Asking for help
Giving help
Offering a kind hand to someone who once tried to break
You
Forgiving them so you can finally forgive yourself
Moving on faster than they thought you should
Falling in love with someone who loves you more than
You've ever known someone could
Wishing things were different
Wishing some things had stayed the same
Wanting back the old life you thought you had
Giving up a life that wasn't meant to be

-There is happiness in knowing what is right for you

Do you see what you've done
Did we somehow make being a book lover
Cool again
Do they want to be like us now
When we were once the loser
We created a mob
A force to be reckoned with
Your photos excite me
Taking up way too much of my time
But I love it
Stacks of books in corners
Current reads
The ever-growing TBR
Multiple options in our bag
For just in case

-There is happiness in documenting what we read

The woman in you didn't just come about
She was created over the years
And years
And years
Be proud that she never gave up
Rest assured that she is trying her very best in
Sometimes, the worst of
Every situation
It's okay to be haunted
To feel like they have all burned you
To be the one thing you didn't wish to be
The time will pass anyway
Like a car changing lanes
And so take advantage of that time
Change your circumstance
Change your mind path
Find and hunt the happiness you deserve
The woman you want to be still has plenty of time
There's so much time
It's not too late to come to a perfect understanding of who
You are

You're only as beautiful as the way you treat people
Remember that kindness is a gift to others
And to yourself
It shatters the walls between you and that person who wants
More from you than they are willing to give
So give grace
Lend a hand
Help someone you didn't want to help last week
They are still waiting for it

I know you'd rather me suffer in misery
But I smile into the sun

My tears are my escape
Everything that I want in this life
Craves me more
I'm grateful that I have created a life that doesn't owe
Anyone an explanation
I've shown you that I deserve the life we dreamt of together
At one time or another
I've shown you in a smile that doesn't come from you
I've shown you in the way he makes me laugh
No amount of Botox can hide the crinkles he puts around
My eyes
Making me happier than I've ever dreamt of being

Empty words are something I won't use
I'll be intentional with what I say to you
To help you to understand
To tell you the truth
About the things you need to hear
About the things you fail to see

At the loss of the bottom
I rise to the top
Like when I think that I'm drowning
But I swim to the sunlight
Air bubbles following right behind me
And I can breathe again
When I felt the beginning of losing you
I thought I was losing everything
Then
I lost you
And I saw then
I still had everything
That
Made
Me
Happy

When I send you off
I only hope you take with you all of the love I have to give
All of the time I've put in
Making sure you are the most confident
The kindest
The bravest
The silliest
Someone who is a product of the things you enjoy
The incredibly endearing heart to explode onto others
I hope you leave me and fold into who you were
Always meant to be
My beautiful son

-There's happiness in being a mother

You're free from my mind
Kind of
Because there's no room here for you anymore
Old me
Same him
You took for granted that space
It's someone else's now
The forward direction I'm running toward
Has nothing to do with the speed with which I push
I'll take my time
Making mistake after mistake
Perfecting the pretty things my hands touch
The things they create
This is not a competition with those who aspire to be me
You shouldn't wish to be me
Be you
Make your own legacy
Break your own rules
Understand your own pain
Push to make your life look like yours
Not hers

-There's happiness in not being green

Shower me in your kisses
Drape me in your love
Am I what you might call pretty
Surely I'm good enough

Why do I question every move I ever make
When it was the world who gave me this incredible stage
I'll do with it as I please
And move within my space
Create me with your own mind
I am not ashamed

You'll think what you want of me
And I'll continue to grow
You may want to be careful
Your words
They're all just for show

-Don't let them take your happy

So far, the things you have survived are all things you
Thought
You
Wouldn't

-There is happiness in being a survivor

All of the money in the world
Will never make you happy

I didn't figure this all out in one day
I knew the time would pass anyway
So I kept going
I kept reaching
I kept my *focus*
I am enjoying my progress
The work I put in
The rip on my heart
The wisdom in my words
See how I speak of these scars he left
I'll be just fine

The wrinkles at the corners of my eyes
As I remember the first two
The increase in the word count as I type this book

-There is happiness in writing

I think sometimes I forget that I don't *need* you
Like, when you fail to follow through
There is a longing left there
In a path
A wake
You don't like when I say that
But it's the truth
I don't need you
I simply want you
And that should be better than needing you
I learned that needing and wanting are two different things
Dangerous, a need
A need from someone is hard to come to terms with
When you no longer have it
It's no longer there
When you need it
There are deep desires
Instant gratification
Unlike a two-day delivery
Sometimes you think you're getting something
And then
It never comes
So it's better to want you

Not need you
Please understand
I mean no harm in it
I have to protect myself

I don't need you, boy
I simply want you

-There's Happiness in Knowing the Difference

I noticed very late into writing this book that I simply do
Not know how to relax
He told me to work on it
So
I
Am

-Happiness is knowing when to take a break

Around the corner is your happiness
Are you going to turn toward it
Or
Will you shy away from it
Afraid of the outcome
If you don't turn the bend

The sun
It crisps my skin
Turning pale landscapes brown
Curbside
I sit with a book in my hand
Reading line for line
The sun
Shining on its pages
Rattan sandals kicked off
Sundress fluttering in the wind

-Happiness is reading in the sunshine

Your happiness shouldn't ride on me either
Were you ever happy with me
Or did you tolerate me
The questions used to keep me up
At night
Currently though
I sleep like a baby

Let's set goals we can achieve
Let's talk better to ourselves

Sometimes I surprise even myself
With how brave
How strong
I can be

Do you know what's funny is
It used to be what was supposed to be the best year of my
Life
I was releasing another book
And as I was gearing up for a book tour
You and her tried to ruin me
Playing games I was never going to win
And so it turned out to be the worst year
But that's fine because my best year was yet to come
I set aside moments of time so I could move on
The escape of it all
The chance to rediscover myself
A moment to redefine myself
An example of how to love myself
A year is just a year
And it took less than that to get over you and the
Spotlight you tried to steal from me
I found something else to find happiness in
I gained a new respect for myself
I learned to see selfishness and narcissism so easily
It was the best thing that ever happened to me
Maybe not for you, but for me... yes
The best thing to ever happen

Float
Float away
Float away doubt

Stop feeling guilty about the things that make you
Happy

I am my own sunshine
Wind through my hair
Peaceful joy
Favorite fragrance
I don't need his touch
I possess my own

Everything you said you would do, pretty face,
You've done
Be proud of that
Be excited at how far you've come
Those who look toward you for inspiration will continue to
Stare
Make it worth their while

-Happiness begins with me

Who are you to make me chase you

Sometimes
When I'm by myself
I sob and wonder how
After fifteen years
You could so easily have closed the door on me
I was your daughter, too
You know
I heard you posted a picture after scribbling right through
Me
Did it help you to forget
Acting like I was never there
Like I wasn't the reason that picture even happened in the
First place
I hid the sting so well
Like it didn't kill me to hear of you trying to erase me
Over and over
I try to think back to simpler times
Where we were kind to one another
I would never have scribbled your face out
And once again I'm reminded
I'm the only one in the room left with her
Dignity

I let the light in and my entire being
Completely
Flooded
Me
My self-esteem is such an important project
It changes everything I touch
I'll focus on that to be a better me
A better mom
A kinder friend
An understanding lover
A determined being

I try my damndest to be everything my ambitions
Push me to be
This racing mind overwhelms my soul
When there are frequently not
Enough hours in the day
It's hard to focus when there are so many
Things to do
And it's hard to remember
I don't have to be everything they
Think I should be
I just need to be me

Sometimes
I have to remind myself
It's okay to be sad
And when I'm sad
It's because I think of having you just half of the time now
I cry alone
In the car
In the mirror
Into my hands
How many kisses will I miss out on
How different will you turn out to be
Now that I only have you half of the time

-I wish I hadn't taken for granted the happiness you give me
just being your mom

Packing up those old ginger jars
Wrapped in thick industrial-like paper
Left a depression in my chest, a gaping hole
Blues in all shades
It was hard to comprehend
All the years I'd spent collecting them
You thought they were junk
But as I unpacked them in my new home
The one I had to get because I couldn't stay
One that was just mine
I thought of how happy it made me
To have them to unpack
Blues in all shades
I'm glad I kept them
And didn't listen to your terrible sense of design

-There is happiness in the things he didn't like about me

The friendship bracelets you gave me
are worth more than gold...

I'll never forget
For the rest of my life
When you drove an hour to comfort
My crying eyes by the water
The boats made their way to nowhere
Tied by buoys in their safe harbor
As I thought out loud things would be okay in mine
This is just a phase I said
Just a small moment of pain
I professed in the sound
And we shared each other's hurts over coffee
As tears fell from my already swollen eyes
I tried to entertain you while dying inside
Setting Bicotti out on little plates like I was hosting a party
There have been moments over this past year
When I thought in silence over and over again
How grateful I am to have two friends like you
To cry with for three hundred and sixty-five days
I know I wasn't the best friend during this time
But I promise to make it up to you

-There are ways to be happy if you surround yourself with
good friends

You're not a cruel fighter for sticking up for yourself
When they criticize you for doing things
That make sense to you
And bring you back to happy

If anything, this year I learned
To find gratitude and happiness
In even the worst of situations
Because if I didn't, eventually all the bad
Would have killed me if I let it
I just couldn't let it
Don't you let it

I'll forever hear her ask me
What kind
Menthol or nonmenthol
I realized I was so clueless
Because I said to her
I'm not sure
What does that even *mean*
Whatever will do the trick
I said
Do you need a lighter
I stood there at the gas station window
Crying like a lost child
And she reached through and said
Whatever it is, it'll be alright baby
And at the time
I didn't believe her
But now
I do

It might seem hard to come to terms with the fact that your
Dreams before
Are not your dreams anymore
Sometimes, dreams change
And sometimes, they become
Bigger
Better
Brighter
Bolder
Sometimes they become
More clear
More justified
More driven
Pushing you toward where you are meant to be
Not where you think you should be

I sometimes like to sit in the quiet
Alone with my thoughts
Especially when there are so many

You are more than the terrible things that have
Happened to you

Try not to let them be all-consuming
For you may one day lose a spark that
No one can give back

Don't be so hard on yourself, dear
You've made it thus far
And that is miles from where you were last year
Because here we are
So take it in
Soak in the goodness that is around you
Remember
You put it there

On that boat floating over the glass
Your note flew from my hands
I gasped so loud that everyone looked around
But it's the little things that mean the most
My heart sometimes hurts at the little things I've lost
And when your note floated away
Sinking slowly into the dark water
I thought to myself *shit*

I keep things in gold frames
Cherish handwritten mementos
They remind me of the love others have for me
Because sometimes
It sure is easy to forget

Distractions only take away from the happiness we are
Meant to achieve
Limit them
Boundaries like an invisible shield
Don't be afraid to use them
Don't feel a second of guilt about them
Look at how they act when you put them up
It'll tell you if you were right or not

That was hell, but I've arrived in heaven.

They seem curious about how much time we need to

heal.

Turns out, you helped me in needing

hardly any at all.

I think of you
And you brought such a simple happiness to my life
That I didn't know I could get back

Her: This was supposed to be the best year of my life...
It's turning out to be the actual worst.

Him: Well, the year isn't over just yet.

-Don't forget that 2022 was a happy year, too

The hours spent laughing with you
Are
Everything.

-Your wrinkles make me happy

I want your books to line my shelves
Not the ones he built for me
But the ones you and I dream up
We draw out the plans
Inspired by those built by others
Pick the type of wood
Decide easily on a paint color together
Maybe a dark gray
A haunting blue
Over the years
Our collection of pages will grow
And hopefully, we won't have to split it up down the road
You always say not to be so pessimistic
But
How
Can
I
Help
It
When I already had to give up one library

If we each go our separate ways...
Let's not think like that
You say
But always in the back of my mind
Is you leaving

But no
Let's not think that way

-There is happiness in daydreaming up a life with you

Mind reader

I can't read minds
But he reads mine
And it surprises me every time

You know me so well
Intentional with every move
Every word you speak
Chosen so carefully
Thoughtfully
And I'll never take for granted
You wanting to work things out
And talk things out
I think it's what I have been missing

I'll overthink this
I really will
I promise
You'll have to communicate well
I tell you every time

-Happiness is when he talks me through

When I met you
My heart was in pieces
Broken like the glass ceiling I tried to shatter the year before
Are you a patented glue
Someone with years of experience putting things back
Together
You say I am your world
Like every little thing
And I say you are mine
Someone who makes my world continue to spin
Just when someone thought he had the power to stop it

-There is happiness in him.

Will there always be?

You ruined the surprise
But it was still
A
Surprise

And still, after all of those lovely moments
I patiently wait for the rest of the surprises
You constantly remind me
That I deserve

This is only the beginning of us
No time at all was used
And yet
I feel like a lifetime has been spent
Laughing
With
You

It's not that I'm devastated
It's just that there's a test
Next to a tampon applicator in the trash
And the emptiness inside me should be filled with a life
Which it's not
So I guess now I just wait with such strife
And for the red to pass and the hurt to fade
And we try again for another twenty-eight days

I should be happy
Grateful I already have two
I try not to think that I don't have two with you
I want more little toes
More kisses on *her* button-nose

You say there's no pressure
But I feel enough for both of us
And I'll try to give you everything we want
If only
If only
Our thousand wishes were enough

I swear, you're my Taylor Swift
I don't want to go a day without you

-There's happiness in Taylor Swift + you

How much time together is too much?

-There's no such thing as too much time
If you're having a good one

The wind blows through my hair as we walk the streets
Hand in hand
You have shown me so many places
It's my turn, let me show you something new
The colorful buildings stand four and five stories tall
The boxwoods
Green, manicured, squared
The peaceful calm of the fountains spilling water
Over and onto
Concrete
The architecture
Vintage and historical
Screaming for us to research it
You keep things so simple
You never ask for much
Grabbing my hand, no matter where we are on the streets
No matter who sees, you want them all to see
Desperately holding onto each other like the love we don't
Want to lose
Adoring wrinkles that connect cheeks to eyes
You radiate happiness like the old cobblestone we walked

-There's happiness in Charleston

The night I lost everything
I somehow gained you

Because of you, I see beautiful things
And I actually notice them now
Before I used to pass by a beautiful garden
And not see the awe in it
The beauty in it
 I used to look up to the sky in the morning
With a cup of coffee in my hands
And not notice the cotton candy clouds
I notice them now

You said in the most beautiful voice
I want it to be you
The one who I come home to every day
In those sundresses I love
I want it to be you
Always

How did I get so lucky to find you

Let me make things simpler for you
It's what makes me happy
From where I stand, happiness radiates from you
There's happiness in the right timing of things that come to
Us
In ways we never thought we'd have again
The things you leave around the home that is now mine
Alone
They bring me happiness

I have found happiness in our routine
It's okay if you don't yet
You like change
I don't blame you
And the waves moving underneath you
You have a hard time believing I didn't have a life before you
Can't say I blame you
I can imagine
It's hard
Watching me move on so quickly
But I didn't though
It took forever
Lifetimes
This didn't happen overnight
I promise
I'm not still in love

How
Can
I
Stretch
The
Time
I
Have
With
You

You say that we have all the time in the world
I just want a darling little girl
Someone who will love me the way that you do
And who will smile all the way up to her eyes like a fool
For all the love we have for each other
You hold me and tell me it'll all be all right
And I believe you
But just for a little while

-There's happiness in solidarity

I just know in my heart
I've never wanted something so badly in my life
I crave her and her laugh
I long for our time together
Our day trips in the sun hand in hand
Brunch in sundresses and nails painted pink
It hasn't happened yet
I think to myself
But I would do anything to have her
Still, that doesn't make her appear
So I wait
Patiently, day after day
For a time when I can call her mine
And we will be *yours*
I urge my mind to stop being so green with envy
I've never been this way
At those who have their *her*
A daughter
It's only you who can make me want something so badly
That I don't already have

-I think there would be happiness in having a daughter
someday

I love your things splashed all over my bathroom
Splayed throughout my sheets
Scattered across my counters
Spread all throughout me

-There's happiness in lightening life up for you

Edit: now your messes give me anxiety, and that is
Something we are working on

I made a board named *Pretty Things*
And on it
Rings
White gowns made of lace that would
With such specific thought
Cover the old tattoos I regret
Rule number one
Do not ink a date or a name next time
Nothing lasts forever
But you say it might

The shadow of the rain pattering at the plane's window casts
Shadows on the pages of my book
You reading next to me
And I think to myself
How did I get you
I look over at you, smiling
I'm sure they all saw me from behind
Admiring you
Thankful you're mine

One road in
One road out
I heard someone say
And it was true
But we circled that island didn't we
And it changed my view of you
In the best of ways
I saw that entire city with you in just a couple of days
On our last night
You took me back to Hemingway's house
So we could slow-dance
To the live music
Played by a band for a wedding
In that courtyard

Again, I fell in love with you
Over and over

I'm reading again because of you
We read so much
On that trip
Turning pages next to each other
I couldn't keep my eyes off of you
Heaven and hell altogether
Heaven because you're mine
Hell because I'm not the pages you touch

-Happiness never faded while we were in clear water

Breathing is easy
It's the after part that is hard
We sat with my hand in yours
Bustling crowds
Too loud to focus on our books
We sat across from one another
Two book lovers just trying to turn a few more pages before
We boarded
I knew every few moments
You subconsciously thought of me
Because your long fingers ran across mine
And I thought to myself
How did I get so lucky to find you
This entire time you bragged to others about me
Even though you were supposed to be
The center of attention
Your skin still dark from our last trip together
Remember the thin yellow slice of lemon that threw the
Cashier for a loop
The sour in my spicy salmon
She was so confused
It's the little things

The way my mind opens up
With you next to me
It helps place a peace and calm in me
The endless possibilities of a new tomorrow
That if something goes awry today
That the sun rising is another chance
For you
For me
For us

I will love you so good

You'll have no other option but to want to place your books
On my shelves

-There's happiness in loving a book lover

My first different kiss in fifteen years
We were so nervous
As I stood, so high on my tippy toes, to reach you
Now, I need a new language to describe how much
I love you

What if I could pick what I dreamt up at night
I thought to myself as I dreamt about you
Is that what I did
Dream you up
I think I'd pick someone like you
Someone who dreams up babies with me
Ones that look like us
A daughter
With light eyes
A delicate heart such as yours

I thought about how much good I deserved
After a year of bad
And then you showed up

Your lips said to me
You bring positivity to everyone who is lucky enough to know You

And it brought tears to my heart because
That's the way I feel about you

I love the angst in you sometimes
If only because I'm the one that gets to calm you
Settle you
Be with you in the gravelly moments
Can I have you for longer than forever
If only
If only

Happy people take chances and leap
You once said
And to my surprise
Our skin turned golden next to each other that summer
I thought to myself
I never really liked the waves
The salt air
The sand in between my toes
But then again, it's who you're with
I suppose
Because with you
The sun could be covered for days
And I would still feel warmth all around
Who needs the sun when I have you

-Happy times occur when and where you least expect them

I'm scared that you're not my permanent thing
Because I have found in the past
I can love something so much
And know still that I should let them go
Whether that may be the right or wrong thing to do
I'll forever know that I'll be okay with the time
I spent with you
Good can come from what you do with the future
The past was a terrible time
In the rearview mirror I can leave many things behind
Like I said
Whether that is the right or the wrong thing to do
I'll be thankful for the time I spent with you
I'm fine to be alone for once
I shouldn't jump so quickly
But steadfast
I jump, I jump
Are you with whom I was meant to be
I quickly find that I search for things
That others don't
A meaning in place
You are what I want myself to convince
That I don't want to replace

I remember falling so hard for you
Will you be there to catch me, too

I couldn't help but cry
When I heard the news at first
They accepted our offer
Our first home purchase
Our first *home* together
I couldn't help but cry
Because I could have done it on my own
But I get to do it with you
Once again
I put my love and my heart and my entire being
In your hands
But this time it feels different
Because we are doing it together
And together
We have all of the love for a thousand lives
I would search for you in any other life
And ask if we could do this moment over and over again

My next chapter isn't missing anything
I have everything left to write
I have everything with you to gain
For what I had before was a placeholder for the next chapter
Pages to be filled with beautiful words
Titles to be named in bold
Characters to be created from love
Found in the least likely of circumstances
You are my point of view
And I love every word that falls from your lips
The way you kiss me is a theme
You plot my demise as we fall into the sheets

-There's happiness in writing the story of us

Our two souls didn't meet by accident
Just like theirs didn't

And I've become grateful for the universe pointing out what
Wasn't mine to begin with
He was never mine
But you are

You gave me something else to write about
And when I'm with you, it never stops
The constant
Trying to memorize you and our moments
I want to pause time enough so I can jot things down
My muse
Thank you

-There's happiness in the moments we create

These seasons are changing
They remind me it's been a year
Time is changing
And that's all I know
It's that time will change me
And change these colors
It's a welcomed change
Both the seasons and my heart
All we know is that the time will change us
We won't stay the same
It should be welcomed

-I'm so happy seasons change

This love affair with you is nothing short of a miracle
Something we both deserve after a year of sadness and
Pure madness
And I just want to be with you
Make a life with you
Hold hands with you and just
Be with you
Even if it doesn't last forever
It was enough to pull us both back to
Where we are meant to be
And that's happy

Book's end

Reader, thank you for taking the time to pick up this book. I hope it made you feel better and more at peace than before you read it. I hope this year becomes lovelier than the last, and if not, that these pages inspire you to pick yourself up and be more kind to yourself. I hope you're gentler to your inner beauty and the outer, to your surroundings and the places you find yourself in. I hope you take circumstances and make them better than you found them. I hope you're proud of who you've become when you look in the mirror. Proud of the things you've created to make your life what you want. And if not, you give yourself grace and time to get there. After all, this is your life. What will you make of it and all it has to offer?

Please share this book if you loved it or think someone else could benefit from its words. Post about it. Write a review on GoodReads or Amazon. Take a photo of your favorite passages, highlighted and annotated. Please send me a note, and pop into my DM's on Instagram so we can chat! I'd love to hear from you!

-S. C. Porter
Instagram: @the_book_lover_book_club_

Made in the USA
Middletown, DE
27 October 2023